Croatia

The 30 Best Tips For Your Trip To Croatia – The Places You Have To See

Traveling The World

This document is geared towards providing exact and reliable information in regards to the topic and issue covered. The publication is sold with the idea that the publisher is not required to render accounting, officially permitted, or otherwise, qualified services. If advice is necessary, legal or professional, a practiced individual in the profession should be ordered.

- From a Declaration of Principles which was accepted and approved equally by a Committee of the American Bar Association and a Committee of Publishers and Associations.

The information provided herein is stated to be truthful and consistent, in that any liability, in terms of inattention or otherwise, by any usage or abuse of any policies, processes, or directions contained within is the solitary and utter responsibility of the recipient reader. Under no circumstances will any legal responsibility or blame be held against the publisher for any reparation, damages, or monetary loss due to the information herein, either directly or indirectly.

The information herein is offered for informational purposes solely, and is universal as so. The presentation of the information is without contract or any type of guarantee assurance.

Contents

Introduction

Croatia, the new hotspot for all types of travelers – the backpackers, the adventure seekers, the honeymooners, and the families – is one of the fastest growing tourist destinations in Europe. It is a magical place, there to satisfy all of your Mediterranean fantasies featuring sapphire blue waters, breath-taking natural scenery, and a rich cultural heritage.

Poised between the Balkans and Central Europe, the country has been colonized and passed between countless of empires and kingdoms, thus leaving behind a rich cultural legacy – from Venctian palazzos, ruined Roman arenas, Byzantine mosaics, Slavic churches and much more, all with the dreamy backdrop of sunny beaches. It is one of the most diverse travel destinations in Europe – you have the Adriatic coast and over a thousand islands to explore, mountains laced with waterfalls, natural parks, seven world heritage sites, islands views, and the timelessness that is observed through the centuries-old architecture seen everywhere, from the ancient walls, to the churches to the ruins. It's a picturesque country, almost "too polished", offering you a chance to experience the beauty of mountains rising from the middle of islands, thousands of KMs of coastline, pebbly beaches, and all the cultural monuments scattered all around the country. Every city will be offering you a new experience...

Zagreb with its contemporary cultural scene, its galleries, and museums, and the Austroa-Hungarian architecture, The Dalmatian coast with its clear waters coupled with oceanfront towns and incredible music festivals, Dubrovnik with its Baroque Buildings, medieval castles, and ancient monasteries, Zadar with its blue waters, its Roman ruins, and of course its seafood, and Istria with its stone alleys and harbors. In the many cities of Croatia, you'll find the Venetian splendor, the medieval and baroque, the Roman ruins, and the splendor of the islands.

Embark on this journey to Croatia, and prepare yourself for its oodles of history, its delicious seafood, the wine, the adventure, the ancient walled towns giving way to azure waters, and the amount of culture you'll be exposing yourself to!

The book will help highlight the top cities you should go to and the top activities you should do in each city, so you could get the full experience out of Croatia and not miss out on any of the important sights!

Geography

Croatia is located in south-Eastern Europe, and shares boundaries with Slovenia, Hungary, Serbia, Bosnia and Herzegovina, along with the Adriatic Sea to the West. This crescent-shaped country has a very geographically diverse terrain. One of the most striking characteristics about Croatia, however, is that it has over 1244 islands in the Adriatic Sea and only 66 of them are inhabited. There are forests that make up 36% of the surface area, there are flat plains along the Hungarian border, mountainous regions with snowy winters, coastal areas and highlands. There are numerous water sources, however, the country's biggest lake is Lake Vrana, while the Plitvice lakes are the most famous – they are composed of 16 small lakes connected by waterfalls.

The geographic features of the country are divided into three: the Adriatic Basin, the Dinaric Alps and the Pannonian Plain, these range from the long coastline in the Adriatic, the mountain chains in the Dinaric Alps and of course, the large lowland and inland region with several rivers like the Danube in the Pannonian Plain.

Culture and Lifestyle

The culture in Croatia is as diverse as its terrain, with different regional cultures in places like Dalmatia, Istria, Slavonia and Zagorija. There is a lot of diversity in the cultures, since they were influenced by may different cultures like the Mediterranean, the central European and the ancient Balkan. This gave birth to three distinct cultures: the Dinric, the Adriatic, and the Pannonian. The cultures are different in terms of traditions, food, folklore and even dialects – however, Croats in general shares a major sense of nationalism. They take great pride in their heritage, and try to preserve it as much as possible through folklore. They feel very strongly, as well, about their regional identities specially when it comes to the food and the language. The folklore is one of the ways Croatians preserve their culture and it comes in many shapes: **Djakovacki vezovi** is a festival that is devoted to a lot of folk traditions, for examples, and '**Kaj su jeli nasi stari**" is a festival devoted to Croatian cuisine, while the **"The Festival of Knight Games"** is there to honor the sword battle dances.

So, they use a lot of mediums to express their nationalism – like poetry, music, and dance, and translate all of the life experience into songs, melodies, myths, and symbolic rituals.

The Croats are also family-oriented people, and the families play a huge role when it comes to day-to-day activities, and the family is the basis of the social structure. People are also quite close to their extended families, and remain close to their mothers and fathers and extended families even after getting married and moving out.

They are friendly, hospitable, outgoing, and it's quite common for strangers to strike up a conversation with people they don't know on the streets, and invite people over large meals at their houses.

Lastly, church and religion play a very important when it comes to shaping the national identity.

Language

The language spoken in Croatia is Croatian which is a South Slavic language spoken mainly in Croatia, Bosnia, and Herzegovina by about 5.5 million people. The language actually dates back to the 11th century, and up until the 19th century, there was no standard written form of the language. The alphabet is based on the Latin alphabet.

English, however, is very widely spoken as about 80% of the population are bilingual. Their TV shows and movies are not dubbed, and are instead in English with Croatian subtitles, making even the non-English speakers more familiar with the language. If you go to the more touristy places as well, you'll find the percentage of fluent English speakers much higher than the small cities.

Religion

Religion has played a main role in shaping the cultural values for a lot of Croatians, and the majority of them identify as Christian. 86.3% identify as Roman Catholic and 4.4% of them identify as Eastern Orthodox.

UNESCO Intangible Cultural Heritage List

Croatia stands in the first place among other European cities when it comes to Intangible Culture. There are a lot of crafts like lacemaking, gingerbread baking, wooden toy carvings, along with singing and dancing traditions. Some of these include the following:

- **Bećarac singing**
- **Klapa singing**

It is a type of folk-singing that comes right from the picturesque beautiful coastline of Dalmatia in Croatia. It's an important tradition there and could be summarized as a group of a cappella performers singing regional folk and popular songs. Klapa is usually sang in groups and can be done either informally in informal settings like bars and houses, or formally in concert venues and as forms of presentations. The groups consist of 4-10 all-male or all-female members, and they sing in harmony together about love, fishing, war, death, drinking and all the other folk traditions. The name *klapa* derives from *capulata* which means a group of people gathered around in the dialect of Trieste in Italy.

- **Kolo dance**

The kolo dance is also very popular in Croatia, which directly translates to "circle" since the dance is often done in circles. It is performed amongst people who hold each other's hands or waists and then dance with their feet and legs – since there is little to no movement above the waist.

When is the best time to visit Croatia?

Weather

The country is divided into two parts with very different climates; the internal part has very cold winters with snowfalls and hot summers with storms, while the coastal park has the perfect mild Mediterranean climate.

The peak summer months of July and August experience the best weather and warmest waters to swim in, however, the prices are at their highest and you'll be walking around in a sea of tourists. The beaches of Hvar, Split and Dubrovnik are perfect.

The shoulder months of May and September have the perfect weather, warm waters and less crowds than the summer months and are an ideal time to visit.

For the months of October – April, head over to Dubrovnik or Zagreb and skip the Adriatic coast since most of the beaches and the resorts will be closed, and enjoy experiencing the local life and skiing.

Important festivals:

April: Zagreb's Cultural season is in April – Contemporary Music Festival and Queer Zagreb Festivals

May: Dubrovnik International Film Festival.

July: International Folklore Festival, celebrating the ethnic heritage with traditional dance and music performances in Zagreb.

Ten helpful phrases to know before traveling to The Netherlands

1. Hello – Bok

2. How are you? - Kako ste? (*formal*) (*KAH-koh steh?*)

3. I'm fine, thank you. – Dobro sam, hvala

4. And you? – I ti?

5. What's your name? Kako se zovete?

6. My name is... - Zovem se _____ .

7. Please? Molim?

8. Thanks! - Hvala.

9. Excuse me - Oprostite.

10. Goodbye - Doviđenja

11. Do you speak English? - Govorite li engleski?

12. Can you help me? - Možete li mi pomoći?

Fun facts about Croatia

- The necktie was invented in Croatia

- It's home to the famous King's Landing in Game of Thrones

- It's home to the world's smallest town called Hum

- Croatia is home of the Dalmatians

- Croatia has the richest collection of the remains of the Neanderthal people in the world.

Zagreb

Zagreb, the capital city of Croatia, is a picturesque city situated on the Medvednica Mountain and one that is usually bypassed since people head straight to the coast. However, Zagreb is one of Croatia's most charming cities, it's the perfect delightful city with a rich culture, lovely architecture, lots of museums, cafes and bars, lots of sidewalk cafes, and quirky little streets you can get lost in. It's a city that will slowly wiggle its way into your heart and make an impression, a city that doesn't strike you as *incredible* from the first sight, but one that will slowly – but surely – will make a lasting impression. The city's walls and streets are filled with streets, as it was shaped by multiple wars and natural disasters, you'll fee the pain, the culture, the purpose, the history, the depth of it all, and you will experience the culture first-hand. Perfect medieval towers and ancient cathedrals are the backdrop of quaint cafes where people sit and sip wine and watch the world pass by while listening to street musicians. It's lively, buzzing and pulsating with energy, it's colorful and most importantly – it is fascinating. From gritty town quarters, to medieval cities, to cobbled streets to the carefree laidback culture of the Mediterranean countries. It's eccentric and quirky, an increasingly creative city that offers one surprise after the other.

The city is divided into three parts: Gornji grad which is the Upper Town that is over one thousand years old. This part contains the Presidential Palace, the St Mark's Church and the parliament, along with museums and galleries. It lies high above a hill and it's more peaceful and quiet than other pars of the cities.

Then there is Donji grad which is the Lower Town – this is the place with all shops, cafes, restaurants, cafes, parks and is more contemporary and new. However, very few tourist attractions exist there. The city was actually once two different city centers, the Kaptol inhabited by the clergy and Gradec inhabited by the farmers and merchants.

Zagreb awaits you, with its numerous cafes, its Croatian dishes, its bars, its nightlife and its historical delights.

Did you know? Zagreb has been called the city of museums since it has more museums per square foot than any other city in the world.

Here are the top attractions you must not miss out when traveling to Zagreb.

Mimara Museum

Out of all the museums in Zagreb, this most definitely has to be the most impressive one, and the biggest in terms of quantity. The Mimara museum is housed in an 1896 Neo-Renaissance building that was once a grammar school, and it covers an extremely wide range of items that span hundreds of locations and time periods. The museum includes all types of art from archeological artifacts to furniture.

Ante Topić Mimara, was a passionate Croatian collector, who decided to donate almost 4000 objectives to Zagreb, which was his native city (despite spending all his life in Salzburg). He lived abroad most of his life, and then donated all the artwork to the city so a museum could be created – however, many doubts about the authenticity of the artwork had risen in the past few years.

Here are some examples of the art you can check out at the museum:

- On the first floor, you can see a large glass collection from Europe, furniture from the Middle Ages, objects from Asia and the Middle East, sculptures from ancient Greece and much more.

- On the second floor, you can check out sculptures by Medardo Rosso and François Duquesnoyare, Auguste Rodin and Jean-Antoine Houdon.

- You can also take a look at the perfect Chinese porcelain and the Delft pottery.

- You can also stroll through the picture galleries on the third floor. Each picture gallery was dedicated to a different era so you can check out artwork from Spanish masters like Velazquez and Goya, French and English artists like Renoir, Degas, Boucher, and Delacroix, and Flemish painters like Rubens and Van Dyck.

Zagreb Cathedral

As you walk down Bakačeva street, you will be met with the overwhelming towers of the Zagreb Cathedral that rise high above the roofs of Kaptol. It is a monumental wonder, the tallest building in all of Croatia, and the capital's most distinct and most visited sight. Wherever you are in the city, you'll be able to see the soaring towers, which reach a staggering height of 105. Hermann Bollé added those towers.

This gothic-style building is a defining symbol, and even though the current Neo-Gothic style to the church dates back to the 19th century, the original church dates back to a much older time.

Zagreb Cathedral is part of a medieval fortress, and it's enclosed by Archbishop's Palace.

Quick history of the Cathedral:

It was founded 1093, and was renovated multiples times due to damage by the sieges, fires and earthquakes. After a 12-year restoration period, the bell towers were created, and in 1990, more renovations were set in motion.

The whole cathedral is like an art gallery, and as you stroll around the interior and the exterior you'll be met with incredible décor and overwhelmingly beautiful art pieces.

You can check out the minor alters, statues, paintings, the stained glass windows that embellish the entirety of the walls of the cathedral, the shrines, the tombs and much more – it is filled with artistic touches.

You cannot miss out on:

- The grave of Cardinal Aloysius Stepinac, who lies inside a glass coffin

- The long inscription in Glagolitic script that commemorates the 1300th anniversary of the baptism of Croatian people.

- The multiple statues all over for prominent figures like St Methodius, St George and St Barbara, along with St Catherine, St Florian and St Cyril.

- Check out the multiple religious paintings by artists like Albrecht Dürer

You can also attend mass since the church accommodates over 5000 people, and the organ concerts.

After you are done strolling around the church and being immersed into its atmosphere and its art, you can walk outside and admire the fountain designed by Hermann Bollé with the statues of the Virgin Mary and four angels.

St Mark Church

This is another symbolic monument in Zagreb, it's one of the oldest buildings there and one of the most visually striking. It's very easily recognizable, and you'll understand why once you see the colorful roof making it the owner of one of the most famous exteriors in Croatia.

The church was built in the 13th century (and some believe that there is a possibility that it dates back even further than that due to the existence of a graveyard found that dates back to the 11th century), however, it has gone under a lot of renovations and the only two preserved items in the church are the bell-tower and the south wall.

One of the most important things you have to check out at St Mark Church is the South Portal, a rich looking, luxurious gothic portal that consist of over 15 sculptures in gothic and baroque styles.

Some of the sculptures are made of stone, while some are made of wood, and the sculptures mainly presented Virgin Mary with Christ, St Mark and the apostles as well.

You'll also recognize the checkered tiles (red, white and blue), which depict the coat of arms of Croatia, Dalmatia and Slavonia.

Mirogoj Cemetery

At first you might be surprised that a cemetery is being mentioned as one of the top sights you have to visit in Zagreb, but this is the perfect blend of history, architecture and nice scenery. It is one of the most beautiful cemeteries in Europe, and just walking along the paths of Mirogoj is relaxing as you stroll down the 500 meters of neo-renaissance arcades under the domes, admire the pavilions, the tombs, and take in all the untold history and stories that lie in this cemetery. This cemetery is perfectly described as an open-air art gallery.

It was founded in 1876 and is on the site of a villa owned by Ljudevit Gaj. After his death, the villa was sold to Zagreb's authorities who enlisted Hermann Bollé to design the graveyard.

The cemetery is situated on the slopes of the Mount Medvednica and many prominent people are buried there, along with graves that belong to people from all types of faiths – Catholic, Jewish, Muslim, Protestant and more,

Do not forget to check out the Monument to Fallen Croatian Soldiers, the Monument to the Yugolsav National Hero, the Wall of Pain, the tomb of the first president of Croatia, and pass by other anonymous graves while the chirping of birds along with the lush rich vegetation surrounds your every move.

Museum of broken relationships

After immersing yourself in all of the history of Zagreb, it's time to check out the quirkiest museum in the city. It is located in the Kulmer Palace in the Upper Town, and was created by Olinka Vistina and Drazen Grubisic.

When they both separated, they decided to collect all of the items that had to do with their breakup and their relationship and put it in a museum, and after the museum toured the world, the final settling place was in Zagreb.

The exhibit is strange, it will stimulate feelings you did not expect to have while on holiday to Zagreb, it will make you think of every relationship you've had in your past and contemplate the ones you'll have in the future.

You'll be able to read letters, messages, check out all the donated objects that were sent anonymous donors, and then you'll get hit with multiple emotions at once – anger, sadness, humor, lust, joy and heartbreak. You will live with the moments with these people, you'll live their joy and their sorrow through the things they have left behind.

The **Rage and Fury** room, for example, has a broken axe and mirror. There's a room dedicated to relationships that ended with death (AIDs for example), or the **Rites of Passage** room about weddings that didn't last too long. You'll find everything from love letters to prosthetic legs, and you'll be met with multiple surprises the more you look.

Dubrovnik

The Pearl of the Adriatic, the most magical, mythical and fairy-tale like city of Croatia, is also the most popular and one of the most perfectly preserved medieval cities in the world. This is the epitome of beauty, a city so blessed with breath-taking views, historic building, natural wonders and a charm like no other. You can come for pleasure, you can come for history, you can come for relaxation – you will find it all in Dubrovnik.

The city was founded in the 7th century and was ruled by the Venetians and the Hungarians, who have both left a visible mark on the architecture of the whole city. You'll be transported back in time to when it was normal to live in a fortified city, with massive gates and soaring battlements.

The sense of awe that will fall upon you as you set your eyes on the pristine blue waters of the Adriatic with a backdrop of limestone mountains, with white streets in the background, baroque buildings everywhere and the ancient city walls surrounding the city.

Everything in Dubrovnik looks like it comes straight out of a postcard with the sun glistening perfectly on the orange-tiled roofs and as the elegant bell towers soar in the sky, it will be like walking through a fairytale. You will never run out of things to do, there are boat trips to take, days to spend by the beach, ancient walls to explore, delicious sea-food to try, and massive gates to take pictures of.

It is no doubt that Game of Thrones, Star Wars and Robin Hood all chose Dubrovnik to be the perfect location for their films and shows.

You can check out the Old Town, which is a UNESCO World Heritage, and a living museum, you can come for the summer music festivals, you can immerse yourself in the perfectly preserved medieval charm, check out the Baroque palaces, go to theatre plays, art exhibitions and visit monasteries.

Here are the top activities you have to do in Dubrovnik!

Dubrovnik city walls

The main attraction in Dubrovnik, apart from the palaces and the coastline, are the ancient city walls. Dubrovnik is the only city in the world that has retained its walls so perfectly, and it will give you the ultimate immersive experience into the past.

The ancient city walls encircle the whole city and the walls were initially built when pirates attacked the city constantly and foreign attacks. They are one of the most important fort monuments in all of Europe, and the first ones were built between the 12th and the 17th century. The walls were so strongly built, that they not only withstood all the incoming attacks, but also the earthquake of 1667.

They are about 2 kilometers long, include over 16 towers and have the best views of the city, its red roofs, its numerous houses, its Old Town, Buza beach (which is a hidden place for swimming and sunbathing), and the Lovrijenac Fortress. You will be encircling the city, peeking down at the narrow alleys, watching people from above, taking in the beauty of rugged Croatian coast and slowly enjoying the most beautiful views of Dubrovnik you can.

You can walk around the walls in about 2 hours, or get down half way. You can check out all the different towers like Minčeta Tower, the Bokar Tower and Fort Lawrence. In addition to this, you can enter the ancient city walls from the Pile Gate Entrance which is the busiest, or the Ploče entrance.

Do not forget to pass by the **St. John Fortress,** which was built in the mid 14th century and was used to protect the old city port from the southeast side. On the ground floor, today, you can find an aquarium on the ground floor and a maritime museum on the upper floor. The **St Lawrence Fort** is reached after a steep climb, and is used as a stage for the Dubrovnik Summer Festival.

Dubrovnik Cable Car

For even more incredible views of Dubrovnik, take the yellow cable car that takes you right to the top of Mount Srd. The cable cars actually date back to 1969, but after getting completely destroyed during the war, they stopped operating it. However, in the summer of 2010 it was restored and now transports visitors again.

The journey to the top of Mt Srd is only three minutes, and you will suddenly be 405 meters above sea level, with dazzling panoramic views of Dubrovnik right under your eyes. You'll be able to see the Adriatic sea, take fun pictures, check out the Old Town from a distance and you can see up to 60 km. The location is so perfect that even Napoleon Bonaparte used it and constructed Fort Imperial there in 1806 due to its great potential as a defensive fort.

You can walk the trail back down the mountain, or sit at one of the panoramic terraces. The panoramic terraces have telescopes, snack bars, a restaurant, and a souvenir shop.

Stardun

Stardun, is the main street in Dubrovnik's old town that stretches from the Pile Gate to the Old Town Port and is considered the pulse of the city. This street is all pedestrianized, and has been the main promenade for the past 50 years. Cafes, shops and restaurants all line the streets and it's the most favorite gathering place for both Croatians and tourists.

Stardun is also called Placa which is derived from the Greek "Platea" which directly translates to "street". The thing about Stardun is that it merges Ploče Gate in the east and the Pile Gate in the West, and then you'll be able to observe the

Baroque buildings that are all of similar height and design. The Baroque buildings were designed this way because they were all built at the same time and they all have a space for shops in their ground floors.

You can check out the Renaissance church of the Holy Savior, one of the only churches that survived the earthquake, or the Franciscan monastery with its famous pharmacy that is considered the third oldest pharmacy in the world. Finally you can check out the Onofrio Large Fountain.

End your night by walking up and down the Stardun as it transforms into a beautifully lit promenade where people sit to sip on some wine and people-watch.

Rector's Palace

The Rector's Palace stands proudly between the Cathedral and the Church of St Ballise, and is an outstanding monument that reflects many different architectural styles. Interestingly enough, many additions and reconstructions gave it its unique shapes as all the different architects had their own vision of how the Palace should look like, and thus the exterior ended up being a bled of different architectural designs that seamlessly blend together. It's a quintessential Gothic-Renaissance palace that has artworks, costumes and domestic objects of that period.

The Rector's palace was home of the Rector who would represent the Republic for a month; at that time he was not allowed to leave the palace at anytime except for business meetings. There was also a brutal prison in the palace that was cramped, dark and dirty.

However, there's a lot you can check out at the palace today.

Firstly, as you go inside through the front entrance, you will find inscriptions that read "***Obliti privatorum publica curate*** " which means "forgetting your private business, concern yourselves with public affairs".

You can check out the multiple exhibition halls on the ground floor to see artifacts from the history of Dubrovnik, or check out a collection of furniture, textiles, paintings, medals, and much more. You can also see rooms that are decorated with furniture right from the 18th century, or admire the artistic paintings, or check out the Rectors study.

Most importantly, you have to visit Dubrovnik Museum which has antique furniture, objects for daily use, paintings, old coins, and much more.

Lastly, the Rector's Palace has exceptional acoustics which makes it a great place to hold concerts during the summer months.

Lokrum Island

Lokrum Island is located only a short ferry ride from Dubrovnik's Old Town and day trips to there are usually very popular. If you would like an escape from the busy tourist-filled streets of Dubrovnik, then this island is the perfect gateway for you. It's an incredible, forested island that includes a huge variety of Mediterranean vegetation, and there are numerous types of plants and streets that cover the island's surface.

You can check out the Botanical Gardens that has a few hundred different types of trees, and subtropical plants originally from South America and Australia.

You can head over to the Benedictine Monastery which dates back to the medieval times, with walls covered in vegetation. It has a restaurant, features giant palms from South Africa and Brazil, and has a display of the history of the island along with a display of the significance of Dubrovnik in Game of Thrones.

You can visit the highest elevated point of Lokrum, which stands proudly at 91 m, giving wonderful views of the whole island.

Mrtvo More is also another attraction that you cannot miss out on. This pond is a result of storms and erosion, and it's pretty easy to swim in.

Split

With coastal mountains rising from the midst of the turquoise Adriatic water, palaces, fortresses, waterfalls, and a wonderful port – Split is a city that reflects what Dalmatian life is really like and how the typical Mediterranean day goes by. It's a lively buzzing city, that is not only a holiday destination, but a place where locals live as well so you can enjoy immersing yourself in the local culture while doing all the touristy activities.

Split is a vibrant port city located perfectly between the mountains and the sea, and it blends tradition with modernity perfectly. You'll find Roman ruins, Venetian alleys, beautiful vegetation and trendy bars and restaurants. The heart of Split lies, however, within Diocletian's palace built in the 3rd century AD. It slowly got transformed from a palace to a vast space with houses, churches, and lots of narrow alleys. You'll be able to walk around the Old Town, enjoy the sight of yachts along the coast, try the pašticada, or even frog's legs, or watch how history mingles with contemporary design as you drink coffee at a café built into the ancient walls of a palace.

Here are some of the top activities you should do in this Adriatic beauty!

Diocletian Palace

The Diocletian Palace is a rectangular building (215 m x 180 m) that used to house Emperor Diocletian for eight years until he died. However, the Diocletian Palace is the only heritage site in the world where people still live and go on with their daily lives in, it is a Roman ruin that has imposed itself on the sity of Split and became a part of its identity, slowly squirming its way into people's daily lives, mixing history with modernity. Walking and living through the walls of the Diocletian Palace is just like living through history, you walk around the multiple labyrinths, the narrow alleys, and one streets leads you to another historical one, but instead of remnants of the fortified town, you find bars, shops and restaurants. It is, without a doubt, one of the best preserved Roman ruins in the world.

The whole palace holds a very close resemblance to a fortress, it is protected by towers at each corner, with the three most important being: the Gold Gate, Silver Gate and Iron Gate.

You can check out the **Marko Marulic** statue, the **Temple of Jupiter,** the **Brace Radica Square**, the **Marina Tower,** the **Split City Museum** which is housed in a beautiful 15th-century Gothic buildings with paintings and weaponry within.

Marjan

Marjan Hill is where people go to climb in the center of Split. It has over 80 routes on the climbing area with overall beautiful views of all of the surrounding islands and this is where climbers of all ages come to have their own rock-climbing adventures. The hill is covered in Mediterranean pine forest and is considered the "lungs of Split" from the enormity of the available vegetation on the hill.

You can spend your day whichever way you want, however, and instead of just hiking you can walk, run, jog, ride a book or even sit and read a book.

The natural park has dozens of park benches that have the perfect city views, where you can also charge your phone for free or drink coffee. You'll be able to see the nearby mountains of Mosor and Kozjak, along with the islands of Brač, Hvar and Solta or even Vis.

You can also visit hermitage caves from the 15th century or a Jewish cemetery, or walk to the Telegrin which is 178m high and gives beautiful panoramic views, or just sit at Café Bar Vidilica.

There is a tennis court, jogging tracks, and even the city Zoo.

A lot of the best beaches in Split are also right below Marjan Hill, and you can reach that easy by bike, or you can visit the Mestrovic Gallery and the Museum of Croatian Archeological Monuments if you're more in the mood for culture.

The Riva

This is most definitely the most important public space in Split. It has the perfect setting, making it not only a pedestrian heaven, but also a gorgeous sight in general. It has the south façade of the Diocletian Palace, the Franciscan monastery, and the Bajamonti Dešković Palace, and the Port Authorities building on the east end.

It is perfect for a morning coffee, an afternoon snack, or an evening filled with drinks, and it has constant entertaining numerous and cultural events like the Split Carnival which takes place right on the Riva.

The Riva is actually 1700 years old and it is *still* being used as the place to meet with friends, walk around, have public events, enjoy the light breeze and admire the harbor views from this waterfront promenade along with the glittering water of the Adriatic Sea at night. You'll never get bored of the scenery as countless yachts, ferries and boats will keep coming and going and will end up keeping you in a nice, relaxed trance.

Imagine all of this, with the sound of traditional music filling the air everywhere around you as you sit relaxing at one of the cafes by the Riva....Perfect!

Saint Dujam cathedral

The cathedral of Saint Somnius was named after Saint Duje who was the patron saint of Split, and was a bishop for Salona, a Roman city that was the capital of Dalmatia back then. After the fall of Salona, bishop Ivan from Ravenna turned it into a church in the 7th century and now it's dedicated to the Virgin Mary while its bell towers are dedicated to St. Domnius. This is the oldest Catholic cathedral in the world that is currently being used in its original structure that it was built in without complete renovation, making it one of the best preserved Roman buildings in the world.

It was actually built AD 305 as the Masusoleum of Diocletian so this is the second oldest structure that was ever used to be used by a Christian Cathedral.

At the building's exterior, you'll find over 24 columns and two lion figures at the base.

Don't forget to check out:

The glass-protected wooden doors created by Andrija Buvina who decorated the door with scenes from the life of Christ.

15th century altar of St. Anastasius created by Juraj Dalmatinac which has *The Flagellation of Christ* – a sculptural masterpiece.

The cathedral's treasury – with a lot of scripts and documents in Glagolitic script, art works, chalices, and more.

Corinthian columns and the images of the emperor and his wife.

The choir furnished in a Romanesque style.

The bell tower of Saint Domnius which stands about 60 m tall and is considered a symbol for the city of Split, and you can even climb all the way up!

Hvar

Hvar, frequently visited by Beyoncé, Prince Harry, George Clooney and many more A-list celebrities, is undeniably gorgeous! It's sunny, it's green, it's luxurious, and it gives you a glimpse of the luxurious island life you've always dreamed of. It's a great day trip you can take from Split to experience this posh holiday destination!

What does Hvar *not* have? Its history dates back to 6000 BC, it offers the posh island lifestyle, great food, warm weather, and beautiful water! It's full of pam trees, it experiences over 2800 hours of sunshine each years, and the island is full of vineyards, lavender, and olive trees. It has the perfect blend of man-made and natural beauty, as the beautiful fields of lavender and the vineyards work their way up the posh city, turning this small fishing villages into one of the most sought-out cities in Croatia. You can wander around the streets, watch the yachts, visit the Stari Grad, the Vrboska, or the Jelsa. You can visit the Franciscan Monastery and Museum where you will find all sorts of historical artifacts like coins, and documents. You also cannot miss out on the Atlas printed in 1524 by Ptolemy or the painting of The Last Supper.

Pula

Pula is a city that lies at the southern tip of Istria, and is one of Istria's most important cities due to its impressive collection of Roman ruins. It has some of the best Roman ruins in Europe which includes an amphitheater that dates back to the 1st century A.D that is still standing until today and is most important attraction there.

It has a pulsing, flourishing life, and there is a growing art scene there thanks to the new exhibitions spaces getting opened all the time like Museum of Contemporary Art of Istria. It also hosts the Pula Film Festival, and hosts multiple major music events like Outlook and Dimensions with cutting-edge DJs and huge crowds every summer.

What you'll definitely notice about Pula is how much of a friendly small-town vibe it's got, despite the tourists there, it's small and calm with a population of 57,200 who are very proud of their city. There are nature parks, seaside cafes, great restaurants, and a lot of music festivals taking place in the summer. Pula has the little medieval hilltop towns, a few national parks with un-spoilt natural beauty, the Temple of Augustus, Forum and of course, the Arch of the Sergi, along with the Archaeological Museum.

You'll enjoy how you can navigate around the whole city in an hour, and you'll enjoy the slow-paced atmosphere this city offers as you surround yourself with a blend of nature and history.

Pula Arena

As you know by now, there is a strong Roman influence on the city of Pula, and the most prominent monument is the Pula Arena. It's a three-level coliseum built in the 1st century AD with stone walls that can be seen from almost any point of the city. It was built in the reign of Emperor Vespasian and it was used for gladiatorial combats until the 5th century AD when these combats were banned. However, convict battles could still be staged until the end of the 7th century when that, too, got banned. The arena could fit 26,000 spectators and today it is only used for hosting events and performances. Down there, there is also an interesting museum which has objects from the Roman times – like contained used to store olive oil!

The arena has four towers, and 15 gates and series of underground passages that were once used by the gladiators. You can tour the halls below where both the animals and the gladiators were held, you can tour the interior, and the exterior.

In the summer months the Spectavia Antiqva event takes place weekly where actors dress up and recreate gladiatorial scenes. You can also try out some garments, attend workshops, or have great pictures taken of you!

Temple of Augustus

This is another building where you can discover more about the Roman past that influenced much of what you'll be seeing in Pula in the present. The Temple of Augustus is the only remaining building from the old Roman Forum which was a central square also built during the 1st century.

The temple was dedicated to goddess Roma and Emperor Augustus and it was actually used in the Middle Ages to store grain, then it housed a Christian Church and then it was used a museum in the 28th century for stone monuments until it was destroyed in the war.

You'll find columns made from marble, and the architrave reads ROMAE ET AVGUSTO CAESARI DIVI FILIO PATRI PATRIAE (to Romans and Augustus, the son of divine Caesar, the father of the homeland).

Arch of the Sergi

Built in the Corinthian style, this triumphal arc was built by Sergi family, who were a very powerful Roman family that had centuries of power and glory. Salvia Postuma Sergi erected the arch with her own money, so she can honor the memory of the three member: Lucius Sergi, Lucuis Sergi Lepid, and Gnaeus Sergi.

The arch is 8 meters high and has been lavishly decorated while the eastern part is left un-carved, because during triumphs people used to pass from the west and the eastern part was out of view of the public.

Zadar

Zadar is the second largest city in Dalmatia, and is one of the success stories of the Croatian Adriatic! It's located in north Dalmatia, and is surrounded almost completely by the Adriatic sea and the mainland area.

Zadar has had quite a turbulent past, it is one of the cities in Croatia that has suffered the most, in terms of bombings (no less than 72 times) and destructions, and yet despite all of that, it not only remains beautiful, but it also is one of the oldest continuously inhabited cities in all of Europe. It has thousands of years of culture and history, and you'll see that reflected in its architecture – Byzantium, Venetian and Austro-Hungarian.

Now, this city, which is more ancient than Split, has become one of the most important tourist destinations in Croatia, as it provides a complex blend of old and new, of ancient and modern – Roman-era forums with trendy bars, Romanesque churches with bustling cafes.

There's also the southern part of Zadar known for its beautiful, calm beaches, its churches, its contemporary architectural installations, medieval palaces, and much more!

There are 15 ancient churches in Zadar, each unique in its own way but Church of Saint Simeon, Church of Franciscan Monastery, and Saint Anastasia Cathedral are three of the most of the important.

You can also check out the Saint Maria Monastery, which contains an exhibition of collections made from gold and silver called "Gold and Silver of Zadar"

Also, don't forget to try out the local drink called Maraschnio which is made from a variety of cherry grown in Zadar.

The daily market should also not to be missed if you want to try out some local fresh produce.

Plitvice Lakes

This has got to be the most popular tourist attraction in Croatia. You'll probably have seen its picture on Instagram or Facebook on one of those bucket-list destination lists, and for good reason! The Plitvice lakes are the single most visited sight in Croatia, and one of Europe's most prominent natural attraction.

All the dreamy keywords cannot make the Plitvice Lakes justice...dreamy, enchanting, alluring, a misty wonderland, a watery heaven, the Garden of Eden? All of these do not even begin to explain the grandeur of these lakes.

They are located between Zagreb and Zadar and they are made of 16 lakes that are connected together by a few waterfalls. There are also parks populated by wild animals like boars and rare bird species. It's a little piece of heaven on Earth, the water is crystal clear and the forested park is colored in different shades of green. As you walk around the footbridges and pathways, you'll be able to admire the rushing water, the butterflies drifting, the color of the sky and the sweet silence and serenity that comes with all of this.

That geographical landscape is called "karst topography" which means that speficic type of rocks those cliffs are made of, along with the combination of water create this landscape that is seen by the lakes.

There are initially 12 upper lakes (Gornja Jezra) and four lower lakes called (Donja Jezra), and to get the perfect panoramic views, it's advised to follow one of the trails called Oštri Medvjeđak vrh which is 889 m tall.

Sea Organ

The Sea Organ (along with the Sun Salutations which will be discussed next) are two of the most prominent monuments of Zadar, and are sometimes more popular than the city itself. The Sea Organ is on the west of Zadar's Riva, and it looks like a few steps that descend into the water, but what makes it so different is the intelligent engineering behind the design. The lower steps allow both air and water to flow in and out in a way that makes them have chime-like notes, reminiscent of whale calls.

Since the sea is always shifting in different ways, no sound is similar to the one before, and it's a beautiful experience to have – just standing there as the LABIUMS play the chords and the tones of the sea and as you take in the *Orchestra of Nature.*

The Sea Organ, along with the Sun Salutations have been created by architect Nikkola Bašić.

You can also go for a swim from the steps of the promenade and still listening to the sound, and you'll end up being hypnotized by the beauty of this modern icon of Zadar.

Sun Salutation

Another quirky creation by Nikola Bašić, this is a 22 meter diameter solar panel in the shape of a circle that is set into the pavement, filled with 300 multi-layered glass panels, and then filled with solar cells under the glass conduction plates to collect the energy of the sun throughout the day. When the night falls, the inbuilt lightning system is set into motion producing contrasts between light, and dark, and an impressive show of colorful lights and shadows.

While you watch that impressive light show, you'll also be able to hear the music from the Sea Organ in the distance, creating an even better overall experience.

Did you know? There's a ring surrounding the installations that has names and numbers that are part of the St. Grisogonus Calendar that have the first documented astronomy data written in Arabic.

The Cathedral of St. Anastasia

This attractive Romanesque cathedral built between the 12th and 13th is the biggest in Dalmatia and has a beautifully decorated façade. The original building was built as a basilica in the 4th century, but the current three-nave design is the modern 12th century one.

On the façade, you will find a statue of a lion to the left and a statue of a bull to the right and these both symbolize Mark and Luke who were evangelists. After that, the main portal consists of a bas-relief of the four apostles. You'll find a status of a lamb, angel Gabriel and Virgin Mary.

The façade in general has three doors and two rose windows, and you can always climb 180 steps to have incredible views of the city over the sea.

You have to check out:

See the marble sarcophagus that contains the relics of St Anastasia

The decorated stalls in the choir

The stonemasonry around the doors.

The high altar that is covered by the stone ciborium.

The remains of frescoes in the side apses.

The Early Christian mosaic in the sacristy.

The statue of Madonna with the dead Christ lying in her lap

The Bell Tower – three floors, decorated with double mullioned windows.

St. Donatus Church

This church has a primitive and simple design, which matches perfectly the Byzantine-era architectural style that is usually sacral in nature. It was a pre-Romanesque church, which was actually called the Church of the Holy Trinity until the 15th century in the memory of a famous bishop called Saint Donat.

It has an exterior cylindrical shape, and a height of 27 meters and that shape is again, very expressive of the Byzantine age in Dalmatia.

St Donatus Church is also one of the few buildings that survived the Mongol invasion in the 13th century, and right now its space is actually used for musical performances due to its incredible acoustics.

There's also an International Festival of Medieval Renaissance Music that is held annually there to make use of the church's acoustics.

Did you know? There are two Roman columns in the church that are recycled from the Forum.

Krka National Park

Krka National Park is another one of the top attractions in Dalmatia. It is a magical place of waterfalls, running rivers, canyon cruises, and beautiful greenery. The Krka national park is named after the Krka River, and although it is quite similar to the Plitvice Lakes, the difference here is that the amount of water is much greater *and* you can swim here. The Krka River has over 17 species of fish including a trout only found in the park!

Of course, the top attraction of the park are the waterfalls that gush down magnificently – including Skradinski Buk falls (which are actually not just Krka's most famous, but also one of Croatia's most famous sights!)

Important Highlights

You can take a boat trip through the park.

Swim in the water!

Visovac

This is a tiny island which was inhabited by Franciscan monks bank in the 15th century. They proceeded to built a monastery, and a church. The monastery was actually demolished and reconstructed again in the 18th century, and it's still there today – you'll be able to find artifacts, a library and some antiques!

Here lies one of the largest bat colonies in all of Europe as well.

Bilusica Buk

This is one of the easiest waterfalls to reach, and it's surroundings are very easily explorable by foot.

Roski Slap Waterfall

The Roski Slap is also another famous waterfall in the park. It's 22.5m high, and it's enormous in size. To get there, you'll need to go through incredible greenery, lush landscapes and...517 wooden steps! But the journey is worth it as you'll end up reaching the thundering waters of the fall in no time and enjoy the rest of your day.

Instead of taking the wooden steps, you can also take the Roman road above so you can perfectly blend in history with the grandeur of nature!

Manojlovac Slap

This is the third largest waterfall, and one that is a little bit hidden, but definitely the most picturesque. It's 59.6m high, and the canyon next to the waterfall is also one of the attractions with vegetation and wildlife all over.

Poreč

An ancient Roman city that comes to life in summer, a popular holiday resort, and one of the top resorts in Croatia, Poreč is a fun little city to visit! You can head to the Sveti Nikola Island for a quick swim, take a boat there, walk the main streets or check out the roman forum there!

Things to see:

The Decumanus is the main street in Poreč and has been the main road ever since the prehistoric times. *Marafor Square* is the previous location of the Roman forum while *The Parliament Building* is now a museum and is a fun way to use your time!

The Northern Fort – built in the 15th century

Kanonika – built in the 13th century, a prime example of Romantic architecture

The Medieval Walls in the wall

Neptune Temple

Round Tower

There are a lot of attractions you can check out, endless shopping opportunities, posh resort hotels, and so many actives going on through the day, you won't even know where to start! You can also check out the beaches by Porec like Valeta Beach, Crnika beach, Donji Spadici and Olivia Beach.

But here's one place you *have* to visit in Poreč!

Basilica of Euphrasian

This basilica is the prime example of beautiful Byzantine art, and one of the most architecturaly complex. It's also one of the best preserved Early Christian complexes in the world, and therefore it was listed on the UNESCO World Culture Heritage List.

The appearance you will be seeing is the same appearance it had back in the 6th century (although it was actually built in the 4th century). This three-nave cathedral was built based on the Early Christian churches following the orders of Eurphrasius of Poreč, whom this town was named after.

The whole site includes a church, an atrium and a baptistery, but the 6th century masterpiece in the basilica is what is really eye-catching. Incredible 6th century masterpieces depicted on the wall mosaics, ones that feature biblical scenes, angels, martyrs and a lot more.

You'll have to keep an eye on the mosaics, you'll see Mother of God Enthroned with Christ, you'll see Christ as the Lamb of God and you'll see saint woman, even the ciborium is decorated with mosaics.

Go to Korcula Town

Rustic, medieval and fortified – these are the perfect three adjectives that describe Korcula. This town used to be called "The Black Island" due to the town being completely covered in dark, dense vegetation, making it one of the greenest islands in the Adriatic.

You'll be walking around historic fortified town that is lined with palm trees, filled with greenery and blooming with history – this town is like a mini-Dubrovnik without the tourists. It has romantic views, beautiful weather, history and the sea – what more could anyone want?

Local men known for their stone-carving skills were the ones who built the city back then, and they did a good job at it!

Here are some of the top things you have to do there:

Admire the architecture of the Old Town and how the walls and towers are arranged. The streets are arranged in a "herringbone" pattern which means the western streets are straight to allow strong summery wind to pass by, and to block the eastern part from the cold winter wind.

St Mark's Cathedral – A gothic-renaissance church (and the most attractive in all of Korcula) features work Marko Andrijić, Jacopo Tintoretto, Ivan Mestrovic, Izvor Oreb and much more!

The Town museum – It's located in the Gabriellis Palace which reflects the 15th century residential architecture, you'll be taken into a journey through the history of the town in this museum. You'll be able to see traditional tasks like stone-carving explained along with ship-buildings. You'll see Edith Streicher's piano, old household objects, stamps, coat of arms and much more!

The Iron Museum

Marco Polo Museum

St Anthony's Hill – Climb 102 steps up the hell so you can reach the 14th century church dedicated to St. Anthony, and enjoy incredible views of Korculan.

Varaždin

Varaždin is the city of the young, the city of music, the city of happiness, of bicycles, of Baroque art, historical monuments, fortifications, museums, and much much more!

It's located in the North of Croatia and won the award presented by the National Tourism Board nine times!

The city is mostly known for its happy street festival – Spancirfest – which is a street festival held in the summer that ignites all types of happy emotions, summery feelings, pleasant vibrations, and serendipity into your heart, and its classical musical festival – the Varaždin Baroque Evenings which celebrate music in the autumn.

Things to do:

World of Insects exhibition at the Hercer Palace (dead beetles, moths, butterflies, and has a gigantic collection!)

Varaždin Cathedral

Its park-like cemetery, where you can have a nice walk, bask in the sun, smoke a cigarette, go on a date...all while in a cemetery.

Trakoscan Castle

This castle looks like something straight out of a fairytale and is considered one of the most visited castles in Croatia with over 100,000 visitors a year. The castle has been renovated several times, and an artificial lake has even been added to add to the beauty of it.

It was originally built in the 13th century, and was used as a defensive fortification, however, right now this beautiful Romanesque castle is the perfect place to explore – to get lost in and to indulge in the fairy-tale vibe of the castle.

The most fascinating room in the castle is the Knights Room, where you can check a collection of weaponry from the 15th to the 19th century, there's the hunting room, the mmusic salon, and of course the private study of Julijana Erdody, along with many more collections.

Miljet National Park

Miljet is a long, thin island but one of the most beautiful and forested in the Adriatic. Its nature is untouched, and it's the perfect place to enjoy the peacefulness and the p pristine beauty of the surrounding flora and fauna.

Miljet National Park borders two main lakes – Veliko and Malo Jezero that stretch for over 4 kilometers, and since there are paths around the lakes, you can easily cycle or stroll around the lakes, kayak at Mali Most, swimming or sunbathe in the warm crystal clear water, hike up the hills, check out the diverse flora, or cycle!

You can also visit the Oydssey's Cave, you can visit by boat, or visit Govedari which is a village built in Western Mljet.

Barac's Caves

The name Barac comes from a local tradition, where a person named Barac was thought to have fought a Turkish giant and defeated him, and thus the caves were named after him.

You can go for a 40-minute underground stroll with a guide so he can explain how this cave came to be, the secrets of the underground world, the history of the cave, and get lost into the mystique of natural formations that took millions of years to create, you can check out the Upper Barac's cave, Dragon's Gorge and the Hall of the Lost Souls. You'll be able to understand how the stalactites were formed over millions of years, where the cave bear used to live, and where the medieval bronze necklace was found in the caves!

Made in the USA
Middletown, DE
17 February 2018